DETOURS

An Anthology of Poets from Windsor & Essex County

DETOURS

*An Anthology of Poets from
Windsor & Essex County*

Edited by Susan Holbrook and Dawn Marie Kresan

Palimpsest Press
5 King St. Kingsville, Ontario, Canada. N9Y 1H9
www.palimpsestpress.ca

Edited by Susan Holbrook and Dawn Marie Kresan. Typeset in Adobe
Garamond Pro, and printed offset in Ontario, Canada.

Palimpsest Press would like to thank the Canada Council for the Arts,
and the Ontario Arts Council for their support of our publishing pro-
gram. We also acknowledge the assistance of the Government of Ontario
through the Ontario Book Publishing Tax Credit.

Library and Archives Canada Cataloguing in Publication

Detours: an anthology of poets from Windsor & Essex County
/ Susan Holbrook and Dawn Marie Kresan, eds.

ISBN 978-1-926794-15-0

1. Canadian poetry (English)—Ontario—Windsor. 2. Canadian
poetry (English)—Ontario—Essex (County). 3. Canadian poetry
(English)—21st century. I. Holbrook, Susan L. (Susan Leslie), 1967–
II. Kresan, Dawn Marie, 1974–

PS8295.7.W553D48 2013   C811'.6080971332   C2013-901182-X

MIX
Paper from
responsible sources
FSC® C004071

Prologue

As the publisher of Palimpsest Press, I began this book in 2010. Like the anthology itself, this project was full of sudden intersections, unexpected turns, and many detours. But in the end, I am thrilled with the results. The scope of work being produced in this region is truly exciting. Like the landscape itself—with its lakes and marshes, farmlands and forests, urban sprawl and southern tip—this collection showcases diversity, ranging from experimental prose poems to traditional lyrics.

I have lived in this area my whole life, and yet I was unaware of the depth of our literary heritage until I started researching this project. Literary luminaries, such as Bronwen Wallace, Joyce Carol Oates, and Phil Hall, have all spent many years shaping and being shaped by the local arts scene. I was delighted to learn that many of the poets included in this book, through multi-generations, have either founded or maintained our literary legacies—through bookstores, journals, independent presses, reading series and festivals.

In an effort to include as many poets as possible, we limited the work to no more than three poems each and then loosely divided the work into thematically related sections based on road signs. Susan and I had a lot of fun seeing how the poems and images would play off each other, such as the "Do Not Enter" road sign next to Mary Ann Mulhern's poem "censored", or the "Roundabout" sign next to Marty Gervais's "Hips". So whether these poets took a temporary detour onto Essex County's winding dirt roads, or their lives seem a continuous roundabout on Windsor's bypass, we hope that this anthology provides the reader with an interesting change in direction that turns, intersects, and meanders.

—Dawn Marie Kresan

Introduction

In 2010 the Ontario government decided to close the tourist information centre on Huron Church Road in Windsor, and move it up the 401 to Tilbury. There's not much to see until the CN tower pierces the horizon, right?

The staff of the centre (now paid by Windsor Essex Pelee Island region) could tell you different, and have convinced thousands of people (dropping in to enquire about currency exchange or a quick route to Niagara Falls) to stay awhile. The detour yields delight after wonder: art galleries, historic underground railway sites, restaurants, a wine route, migrating hawks and warblers, trees weighed down with Monarchs. And the poets, the poets!

I had already lived here (at Point Pelee, where the trees are weighed down with poets) for over a decade when Dawn Kresan invited me to help edit a collection of Windsor area talent, so I knew we'd have no shortage of material. But even we were surprised when our initial idea of "12 Windsor Poets" rapidly grew to "15 Windsor Poets," then 20, then 25, then we thought we'd better leave the number out altogether. Even as the anthology ballooned, we knew we couldn't accommodate all we desired. There could easily be a volume two, three, four.

One way to narrow down the pool was to demand that all included must have lived here for at least five years. Beyond that we wanted to showcase the eclecticism that characterizes our region: the traditional and the experimental, the academy and the community, the historical and the emergent, the internationally renowned and the promising apprentice.

Gathering materials was a more joyous adventure than I anticipated. Hired at the University of Windsor in 2000, I was fortunate to meet beloved professors and writers John Ditsky and Peter Stevens, who have since passed. Had I not been part of this project I'd never have had the pleasure of hearing Sue Ditsky read her husband's poetry over the phone, or sitting in June Stevens's living room, sifting through Peter's books, June and their son Martin reciting and chuckling over the late poet's wit. I also came to know writers I hadn't yet encountered, thanks to the enthusiastic readership that is the writing culture here.

It seemed every poet we approached would say "What about x?" or "You should ask y" or "The collection wouldn't be complete without z!" The writers in *Detours* are a gathering of lights, forming multiple constellations through a range of overlapping connections fueled by a mutual commitment to writing and sharing poetry. You'll even notice some intertextual camaraderie, as mentors appear in the poems of their students.

We did not seek out a thematic centre, the proposed cohesion borne of poets from a place rather than poems about a place. But we admit to developing a soft spot for poems featuring local geography, from the rocky shores of Pelee Island to the factory floor.

We hope you'll enjoy whatever route you take through the book. Stay awhile.

—Susan Holbrook

Bronwen Wallace

Lonely for the Country

Sometimes these days
you think you are ready
to settle down.

This might be the season for it,
this summer of purple sunsets
when you stand in the streets
watching the sky, until its colour
is a bruised place
inside your chest.

When you think of settling down
you imagine yourself growing comfortable
with the land and remember the sunstained faces
of men like your grandfather, the ridges of black veins
that furrowed the backs of their hands as they squared
a county boundary for you, or built once more
old Stu McKenzie's barn exactly as they'd raised it
60 years ago.
You watch the hands of the women
on market days, piling onions, filling buckets
with tomatoes, their thick, workaday gestures
disclosing at times
what you think you recognize as caring,
even love.

Bronwen Wallace

At least that's how it looks
from outside and when you think
of settling down, you always think of it
as a place.

It makes the city seem imaginary, somehow.
As you drive through the streets,
you begin to see how the lives there look
as if they had been cut from magazines:
a blond couple carrying a wicker picnic-basket
through the park, a man in faded brown shorts
squatting on his front lawn
fixing a child's red bike.

You wish you could tell yourself
that this is all too sentimental.
You want to agree with the person
who said, "There's no salvation
in geography."

But you can't
and you're beginning to suspect
that deep within you,
like a latent gene, is this belief
that we belong somewhere.

What you know
is that once you admit that
it opens in you
a deeper need.

Bronwen Wallace

A need like that loneliness
which makes us return again and again
to the places we've shared
with those we can no longer love,
empty-hearted, yet expectant,
searching for revelations
in the blank faces of remembered houses.

As wide as bereavement
and dangerous,
it renders us innocent
as mourners at a graveside
who want to believe their loss
has made this holy ground
and wait
for the earth beneath their feet
to console them.

Dorothy Mahoney

LaSalle Woodlot

in the morning of hammering
birds call
through the woodlot
full of white trillium
and jack-in-the-pulpit
while the wind toys with
orange ties on stakes
that mark this for clear cut
and the men on the roof
shade their eyes
and look to farmers' fields
beyond this surveyed land
anticipate subdivisions
their jobs secure
for a few more years
while we hunt with shovels
for trout lilies and tulip trees
walk gingerly through thick ferns
study every sapling
oak leaves speared to the dark soil
by small shoots
we speculate at species
boxes and bags heavy with dirt
red baneberry and false solomon's seal
wanting to save everything
wanting to replant this world

Phil Hall

Ruthlessly Local

If I have to hear one more time
about the light from the star that's dead
 or about the full moon's pull on a puddle
I'm going to shut down my observatory
 & turn ruthlessly local

there's a look the elderly get
 when they're eating soup—a reptile
focus—the tongue protrudes—the mouth puckers
 & blows—it's disgusting such devotion
but attractive too because for that moment
 the spoon is the moon

the idea dies
 then the animal inside the idea
crawls out & clings

Detours: An Anthology of Poets from Windsor & Essex County

Salvatore Ala

Unloading Watermelons at the Windsor Market

It took two men and three boys
all day to unload four thousand jumbo watermelons
off two eighteen-wheelers that had just come up
from a watermelon patch in Georgia.
By the end of the day they were so heavy
you couldn't feel your hands,
but we dropped thirty out of that many.

For the first time I was working with men.
The men sang Sicilian folk songs
as they heaved into the load of melons,
and I worked to the rhythm of their rough voices.

Nothing quite so red and wet and cool
as a cracked open watermelon on a summer day,
so hard and green a shell
to hold that much water and light.

Eugene McNamara

Punching In

the coal silo moves the clouds
and i have to climb the silo the
grease gun against each rung as
i climb my eyes on the deltas of
rust running from each bolt in
the concrete and i go up and then
on the top the whole sky opens
and soars now the grease gun to
the conveyor's nubs and a snake
of new grease hangs from the gun
drops to the silo's roof and on
the noon height sudden the air
is full of whistles answered by
church bells and from the national
baking company the smell of bread
and i stand and turn in the singing
air filled with hunger and joy
joyful hunger ringing singing

Peter Stevens

Through Put

My work day lasts eight hours.
You wait at home.
I write a poem—it takes me eighty minutes.
We eat for half an hour.
We make love for an hour and a half.

My love-day lasts eight hours.
You eat at home.
I eat a poem—it takes me an hour and a half.
We make eighty minutes.

My poem waits eight hours.
You make love at home.
I work—it makes me eat.
We write for eighty minutes.
The day takes an hour and a half.

My home does not write.
You eat the day.
I make love to a poem—it takes eight hours.
We work for an hour and a half.
We wait for eighty minutes
                forty
                twenty
                ten   . . . .

The day works us for eight hours.
The home eats us.
No poems wait for me to write.
Love does not take.
We do not last.

Marty Gervais

The Kid

For W. O. Mitchell

You entertained my kids
with magic tricks—
disappearing quarters
found behind the ears
cards that floated in
the emptiness
above the dining room table
You would sit with my
seven year old son
and watch the games on
television, show him
how Lafleur could
cast a spell over the Forum
as he sped over the blue line
a slap shot like the finality
of heavy equipment crashing
to the floor
And a few years ago
you asked my boy
if he would go on television
with you for a Christmas
show where you would
read from a short story—
terribly shy, he ran off
to his room, eyes
full of tears

Detours: An Anthology of Poets from Windsor & Essex County

and you spoke to him
"What is it you want
the most this Christmas?"
"Bauer Supreme skates!"
he said after a moment
"You got it!"
And you went back
to the station and
told 'em to write it
in the contract
And that Christmas
the skates were under
the tree
from W.O.
A month later
you were there in the
arena sitting
in the frozen seats
to watch my son—
cheering him, bellowing
out "Those are the skates
I got him!" as my boy
popped in five goals
and there you were
everybody knowing you
the shock of white hair
voice booming in the arena
my son floating like
his hockey hero—

Marty Gervais

firing from an impossible
angle, the puck
sailing into the net
like a punchline
at the end of a poem
Twelve years later
I'm at your house
They've wheeled
a hospital bed
into the kitchen
Now you lie as silent
as a stubborn dog
and no matter what I say
you say nothing
nothing at all—
until I mention
my boy, how he's
playing in Czechoslovakia
and your eyes brighten
a half smile—
And though you say nothing
I can hear the cheering
in a cold winter
across the ocean.

Detours: An Anthology of Poets from Windsor & Essex County

Alex Gayowsky

Anosmia

i

The school gym smells like exercise must smell like sweat and sneakers squeaking against the floor. Laundry smells like meadows smell like a hot cup of Ovaltine tastes. A corridor smells like the moors sound like the inside of a seashell feels against your ear. A wet dog smells like sulphur smells like a sleeping troll snores in an underground cave. Sharpened pencils smell like a book sounds when you first open it. Baby's Breath smells like a tire swing smells like finding a hidden door inside a fence. Rain smells like freshly laid pavement smells like roof shingles sticking to the bottom of your feet. Sometimes rain smells like forests smell like apples sound when you bite into them.

ii

At daycare we learn how to smell. Mme. Rita and Mlle. Natalie blind-fold us and we stand in a row on the masking taped Xs on the hardwood floor. I'm fifth from the beginning. Or seventh from the end depending on where they begin. Either way I figure I'm okay because I won't have to go first. I want the blindfold to be made of something distinctive. Silk or nylon perhaps, but I can't feel anything on my face. Maybe they don't blindfold us at all. Maybe we're just told to close our eyes. Squeeze them really tight so that we don't peek.
Vanilla, good. Bravo! Peppermint, mmm yes, good. C'est correcte! They clap. The object is revealed. I squeeze my eyes tighter. If I unclench at all, even just a little bit, they'll open all the way and there will be nothing I can do to stop it. I wouldn't be able to close them again. My eyes would stay open forever. Did he say dirt? That's not right. Wood chips. Ah, oui oui. I'm next, now. An insistent clock ticks beneath my ribs. That smells sour,

a voice calls out beside me. Like lemon, yuck. Très bien! I take inventory. Vanilla, wood, lemon. What was the second one? Cinn- no. Peppermint, that's right.

A hand is placed gently across my eyes. It's my turn. What are some smells people smell? Perfume? Coffee? Chocolate? Why haven't I been taught before? It would be nice if it were chocolate in front of my nose. Chocolate smells like honey tastes like a warm cup of milk feels the same as a warm hand holding my face. Beneath, my eyes open, lashes tickling her palm and all I see is glowing.

iii

School tastes like an eraser tastes like old pencil sharpeners wind like lead shavings smear across your fingertips. A bonfire tastes like cinnamon hearts taste like stones getting stuck inside your shoe. Spring tastes like strawberry jam tastes like rose petals feel against your skin like finding a four-leaf clover in the playground at recess. Mountains taste like ice cubes taste like the word 'abyss' feels inside your mouth. A train tastes like cans of Coke taste like velvet feels against the left side of your face. Home tastes like corn on the cob tastes like a towel feels right out of the dryer like a nightlight glows in the hallway.

Nicole Markotić

The mask off, but the mitts on:

Gelati and Canadian Tire, or a missing hedge, or three bets past

        a cone and one cup.

Holidays for mid-week. Who says being a wimp doesn't pay?

                Fleck it, or feck-it

      former dairy plays fort

a fleck of the feelick, a dice of the trice. Whyn't you treble, whyn't you play nice?

Don't stop for the soy-train, the gravy keeps comin'

        why-n-dot: street names for tunes.

I've explained and explained, but dying won't hunger

      just like   gifting for beginners.

Trade union station offers mini-donuts and Rah-rah-Rasputin raspberries

       who know what text's next

             the hunted more than the Huns
won't sneeze for the pope?

Pass the mike, pass the class, pass the tenth of the twelve

      matching shoelaces
      stringing an instrument apart

               why-n-ot?

Ravine

Glee bee
bumble
rumble bee
be!

Pepperfilled thimble
glee bee
bumble
rumbles be.

Glee on the edge, ravine
looks over ravine
ravine oh bee
ravine mad

glee bee
bumble
rumble bee be
bee ravine mad about ravine.

Ravine bee.
Bee ravine.
Ravine glee
bee bumble rumble

be!
Pepperfilled thimble sprinkle
bee ravine
glee.

Glee on the edge, ravine
glee on the edge, ravine glee
on the edge ravine
bee.

Darryl Whetter

Sex: The Selfish Gene, The XX and a Bottle of Shiraz

We do not even in the least know
the final cause of sexuality.
   —Darwin, 1862

why the beast with two backs
when reproduction worked
fine with just one?
mitosis for millions of years,
genetically just
your own ass on the copier

stretch your arms wide
for life's history.
sexless bacteria
alone from your right fingertip
past your left shoulder.
nuzzling and the painted mouth
elbow in with complex plants

three theories on the origins
of sex, this recent sweaty
sideroad in the evolution
of evolution. not porn,
wine or boredom but

Darryl Whetter

the good

      crossbreed our strengths.

      pity the purebred dog (or prince)

      carrying his palsied haunches

the bad

      assassin panties.

      shag to clear the line,

      get the glitches

      out of our gitches

the ugly

      bonking in the parasite shadow.

      our arms race against

      adaptable invaders. the thrust

      and moan to scramble

      the code, cover our tracks.

      a cunning defence

      working your fly

Emily Schultz

Down Bear Line

The colour of this dusk makes a hole in my mouth,
leaves me open and without words. Driving, the wheels
hold steady though I am wobbly—surrounded
by broken-down industry, rust-coloured, dusty farmland green.
Here is the river full of duck blinds where a boy told me
(waiting for darkness to kiss me) that it was fun to kill.

Where is the old dirt pull-off by the railroad tracks
where that hunting boy removed my blouse, left his kiss red,
welted, on my chest, and an invisible disease inside my skin?
I remember girls disappeared at fourteen, swollen thick
as ditch bulrush, giving birth, then continuing their thin
young lives who knows where.

I remember counting amber bottles: the kind of counting
you do when you want something to be over sooner,
something to be closer or farther away. Our families
slurred the things that meant the most, or buried them
under heavy drunk tongues. In cigarette-coloured rooms,
we learned this language, practised to perfection.

Each row of yellowed corn recalls a leaf cut,
flicked quick into thumb crook the July I pulled tassels
for cash to get to university, to get away.
Thorn rain and mud that clung—soaked
its mulch scent through shoes, socks, gloves;
the itch of sweat by blue afternoon.

Emily Schultz

Detours: An Anthology of Poets from Windsor & Essex County

In the city you can forget what building was what before.
Nothing falls into itself. Everything is pulled down
and put up new. A whole block can be erased
in the rain, a single season, and the memory too.
But here, the ochre-grey light gets everywhere.
Runs its hands over everything:
the ditches, barns, bridges, old cars waiting to be restored.

Even the places that are no more appear like apparitions
in the gold-mauve glow of evening—
the house of my first real love, disappeared amid TV static
under the watchful eye of a white dog. A space
left in the world between it and its neighbour. Wind and grass.
And here's the silo we used as a landmark to turn...

Down Bear Line, we put pedal to the floor, stupid
though we knew it, as fast as the car would let us go,
as far as the needle would dip, bury. The starry blur
of road, amethyst of sky, brown of fields, and then
the slow-down, thrill whistling in our chests, hearts still a-rush:
of no one knowing, of not having been caught.

Still, I am caught.
The night sky bends down over the road now
like an orchid. It's dark and there's nothing
here except everything that is here.

Vanessa Shields

The Kinda Girl

she's the kinda girl I stare at from afar
watch the way her boobs bounce firmly beneath braless black

the kinda girl that works all day to party all night
she's the kinda girl husbands flirt with in front of their wives

we sit back and watch in jealous surprise
then ask her to fetch our dessert

she's the kinda girl I secretly always wanted to be
bold in braless braveness

drinking hard smoking chains
she's the kinda girl I finally met

her eyes heavy with booze
her body sexy with languor

Do you love him? I ask
she stumbles over words spinning in her head

out of her liquored lips answers
I don't know

pouring out confidence
she's the kinda girl who I think knows everything

but her eyes close when she answers and
I realize she is alone

Joyce Carol Oates

Detours: An Anthology of Poets from Windsor & Essex County

Love and Its Derangements

They are always trying
to drag me by the hair, away

my skull prickles wisely
at the sound of their footsteps
they want to sink
into me the length of their
bodies   as into an enemy
with a sister's face

they want to learn from me
certain cries and names
they want the music rising to a shriek
they want the river's white sails
to collapse into the dirty water

always
the circular bones of their necks are alive
with desires unworded
always they lean their elbows onto tables
in a code of male conspiracy

they want the new grass
to suffocate beneath the newer seeds of trees
in a hot spring flood

Joyce Carol Oates

Detours: An Anthology of Poets from Windsor & Essex County

in this hot May sun
the line is abrupt between male and female:
shadows of a million swinging leaves
across the inert grass

if I could turn outward
into the flat white walls
of the rooms we use
I would witness a body
at its fate tugged by the moon
all the inches of its skin
rubbed raw with the skin
of men

Stephen Pender

Wish

We muscled out of necessity
into a wish: feeling that feeling
is feeling, again itself, its autumn light
making a fragile dusk, some other,
other season, searching its ends.
How often have we said 'yes'?
How many seasons watching?
From necessity to need: embers
and others, sorry, wishing feeling
into feretories for a coming age.
I wrote to you about saints, but saved
other talk for betters. Now, seasons
and affections, their failings, are what
makes making making still. So we sat
and chatted about evening, wishing
a day into its light, and watched.

Detours: An Anthology of Poets from Windsor & Essex County

Kate Hargreaves

Hip to be Square

Her hips sink ships. Her hips just don't swing. Her hips fit snugly in skinny jeans. Her calves won't squeeze in. Her hips check. Her hips cash in on the market for skin. Her hips max out their credit. Her hip-replacement value is greater than that for knees. Her hip socket pops out on the way up the stairs and back in on the way down. Her chiropractor takes the time to crack her hips. Her hips show through her slip. He slips. Hips shoot from the her. She shoots from the knee. Her hip-to-hip, toe-to-toe, or cheek-to-cheek. She toes the line. She hips the other cheek. Her hips print bruises on the wall. Walls purple her hips. Her hips yellow-belly. Her hips run. Her hips send a note threatening not to return unless working conditions improve. Her hips make the rules. Her hips call her gutless. Her guts call her hippy. Her hip flask calls in sick. Her rose hips. Her daisy dies on the windowsill. Her hips move home in steps. Her steps crack her hipbones. Her hipbones give whips. She de-bones thighs. Her thigh-highs slip. She's a sight for sore thighs. Her thighs join at the hip. Her hips end with thighs. Her ends are split. She splits her hips.

Nicole Markotić

Detours: An Anthology of Poets from Windsor & Essex County

sons and nets

yes, word-play still persists, yes yet

formica as dedication or devolved votes or keener

hasn't there been enough rain to outlast the decade? the decadents want more

     a beam of bookworms, slithering towards unstitched hems

whyn't you call? over the moon, over the clover, over-easy. just: over

a special or a spec
tackles the underline
wrestles the xmas wreath

     who isn't mourning a coffin-sized newspaper?
     last one home is an empty nest
     messy, but effective   nosy, and primal
     a word isn't sums isn't smut isn't mutter

yes

it is what you say, what you pray, what you breach inside the work canal
and ending sl
because the brill ants
plod on   up hill
down slopes the fair
dow nope the flairs

yep

Nasser Hussain

consumer, meet enema

yes i want to
receive sales information

oh yes i want to receive sales
information

so yes i
want to receive sales information

I want
sales information
by email
by text message
by pony express
by by bye
(the way some people say 'bye-eeee')

is this connection slow?

by now, i'd have the slaes informatino
er, the sleas information:

take my pin take my security number take my details
(you're not just dealing with me but everyone in my search history)

five-star rating, would do business again and again and
again until we are more than just paypals, but friends.

bark odes, last day,
everything must
go.

Tom Dilworth

Satin

With thanks to a student who wrote that
Young Goodman Brown is 'tempted by Satin'.

How could Eve be tempted by Satin?
A fine cloth but not as light
or smooth as air
or prelapsarian skin.

Did she wish to astonish Adam?
make him stare or
wonder what's under?
though he already knew.

Maybe paradisal nights grew cool.

Or she fell
for the fashion of all in Eden
that shone like satin,
    pelts of otters and big cats,
    skins of fruits and snakes,
    eyes, wet stones,

wet anything.

train track

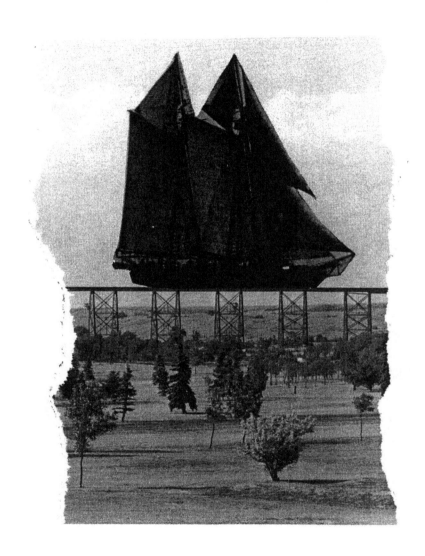

**midnight grocery shopping after watching days and days of
viking week on the history channel**

grocery carts
would not make good long boats:
too many holes.
a disabled freezer chest
in aisle 5 provides
a cold sea to wade through,
and i do, with large, heavy steps.
tonight i would be satisfied
with another man's woman
thrown over my bulky shoulder.
her name would be helga
to my sven.
barring a lack of women to abduct,
even a large fish to char would be nice.
instead, i am left with a tin can
of tuna–dolphin-friendly at that.
i throw the can
into the cart with more muscle
than needed.
an elderly lady hovering
beside the green beans
clutches
her pink sequined purse
tight to her sagging chest.
overripe tomatoes fall
from her gnarled-root hands,
explode, then bleed
onto the cool green linoleum.
i smell blood
and like it.

Mary Ann Mulhern

censored

a library shelf
in the novitiate
has a paperback
on marriage
the chapter on
conjugal love
sealed with
masking tape
words hidden
like full breasts
under layers
of tight binding

someone has
peeled back
brown tape
opening a forbidden
passage

Detours: An Anthology of Poets from Windsor & Essex County

Robert Earl Stewart

Field Notes Towards a Deeper Understanding

The moon was like the residue of sale-price sticker peeled from a pale blue
album cover—and I was the first delicate creature of the spring.

The broken cookies fell from the blue monster's mouth, uneaten—
and this was the first hard lesson about puppetry.

Mrs. Randma's wig rolled like a wheel seeking a shave beneath the speeding
fire engine as we stood apple-cheeked in the fall wind—
this was when "embarrassment" first entered our vocabulary.

A half-eaten Caramilk tucked in my report card and tossed out the window
of my grandfather's Omni northbound on Campbell Street—
and I learned that a misguided gesture can have unintended effects.

It was the day—no, the hour—of ripeness …
and we filled plastic grocery bags with peaches from Mr. Hickey's tree.
Wasps did not swarm around our ankles or heads because not one peach
had fallen to rot in the tall grass, but I barely made the bike ride home
from eating too many in the picking—
and perfection became a liquor too sickly sweet.

The girl who asked me to the prom and left the party in tears, intact—
it was possible, I saw, to be too much the gentleman.

I dreamt I was fitting small songbirds with suits
of custom-designed armour—and learned not to spend the moments
before a nap studying *Sibley's Field Guide to Birds of Eastern North America.*

Robert Earl Stewart

Detours: An Anthology of Poets from Windsor & Essex County

I didn't burn out my arm throwing curveballs because I was not allowed
to throw one. I burnt everything else out though,
in a big dark somnolence of the soul—the last lasting lesson at the bottom.

I was the first delicate creature of the spring. I was stalked by wolves,
followed by bears, and flushed from hiding like a deer
by an inebriate tribe and their quiet "Darts" incantation
and the realization upon waking
that I have a responsibility to the night.

Emily Schultz

The Thing Defines Itself

I am a soul in the world: in
the world of my soul the whirled
light / from the day

—from "The Invention of Comics,"
Amiri Baraka (LeRoi Jones)

The sound of sky is the sound of sky
reflected on the pavement,

the light that blinks,
the open image flung from our window.

The word is night,
the word that rises to your lips
is night, the word of the thing
it is, itself, is night
and the sound is
coarse and shimmering
as fallen leaves beaded with rain
and night.

That is all.
Night is night.

Night is night. You say it, I swallow it,
the sound, the long night Longing slips
out of its dark, old hand of lines.
The sugar-quick flick your voice pulls
slow through me, flickers high

Emily Shultz

Detours: An Anthology of Poets from Windsor & Essex County

out the other side as if you might
slip into the thing you define, small body full
of the word, repeating its meaning.

And my ears full
of reading its hearing.

Your voice is the lid
on the lighter you grip
between your fingers and thumb
click click, the clasp you open and close
for its opening-closing,
for no other meaning but this—
click its opening,
and click its closing.

The sound of you is the sound of you
shivering under the click click

of words and rain
in the night, is night, is night.

Peter Stevens

To Each His Own Ann Landers*

Letter 1: Mr. Snodgrass, my two year old rat,
          has learned to appreciate the many
          benefits of "grass" as I do.
          He eats it.
          He hasn't missed
          one of our pot parties for months.
          Is it safe to assume
          it's as harmless for a rat
          as for humans?

Letter 2: Where Could I sell some bicycle parts
          frames
          and also an old English bike?
          What can I do about acne?
          Is there any way to clean
          old, dried paint and enamel from cloths?

Letter 3: The other day we had a sonic boom
          that scared my mother out of her wits.
          I checked my tropical fish right away
          but I couldn't tell
          that they were bothered by it.
          Are they?

*All letters found in the Windsor Star, June 24, 1972

Salvatore Ala

Detours: An Anthology of Poets from Windsor & Essex County

Visions of a Country Road

On each side of the country road
lean tall old trees far into their shadows,
and you feel a desire to turn off
into the landscape of yourself,
to the end of a road that never ends…
and all that solitude yours.

Go deeper, to where fence posts end,
beyond the rusted out car
now stranded in vines,
where farm land becomes meadow and woodlot,
and the meadowlark is a clear song
of space and light.

There the footings of house
fill in with wild grass and flower,
like house built by the rain,
and shining through itself
a wild barn becomes a holy place.

The deep rustling of the trees
and swaying shadows on the road
call us from our destination
to a landscape beyond the highways,
and the nowhere of being lost.

Marty Gervais

Detours: An Anthology of Poets from Windsor & Essex County

The Cow on the Bardstown Road

A man rides a truck
ahead of me from Bardstown
a cow in the back
shifting back and forth
with each new curve
of the road
its unsteady cow legs
doing a moon walk
on this clear afternoon
in March
I think of its sad cow eyes
drinking in the coming
of spring, of lush pastures
of blue skies
cumulus clouds
the warmth of earth
I think of its sad cow mind
speculating about change
and maybe about
the men and women
in the cars queuing up
behind this truck
and maybe about the
physics of speed
and sound and wind
along this road

Marty Gervais

I think of its sad cow eyes
dreaming of the earth
rushing by without her
A man rides a truck
ahead of me from Bardstown
adjusting the radio
heedless of the traffic
dreaming among the curves
of this road, eager
to bring home his new cow
eager to embrace
the security of spring

Darryl Whetter

Detours: An Anthology of Poets from Windsor & Essex County

Country Dog

real-estate baron,
in a field he is
the incarnation of field.
his cutting, racing
figure eights, feints and
about turns in tall grass
a hockey game against joy

summoned or coaxed to the scratched
back door he carries
seeds, the smell of wind and
the temperature's date stamp
in his fur. burrs and leaping
insects latched with the barbed
malice of a computer virus

sheriff of the domestic lowlands
each half-floppy ear a catcher's mitt
for the distinct plunk of itinerant food.
paratrooping carrots, sandwich emigrants
gravity's scraps

desire on four legs he
animates the rooms
routinely visits the provinces
of nook and expanse
leaving warm oblongs of floor,
tumbleweeds of hair

Darryl Whetter

in angled stretch, diagonal
sprawl or insistent stand
he is enormous, equine and then
enfolded, a black muff
beseeching both my hands
or a comma curled,
life's hairy pause

the winter in his beard
is my discontent
the clicking ratchet of one hip
or glaucoma's indicting blue fingerprint
on each eye of my animal self.
mortality's mute
shaggy ambassador

Tom Dilworth

Detours: An Anthology of Poets from Windsor & Essex County

Not a Wake

When is a wake not a wake?
When it's your 40-year high-school reunion.

I have seen none of them since we were 18,
strangers with familiar names on nametags.
Astigmatism in the cornea of time.

An experience too strange to assign to similarity,
but let me try.
like a child soaking in a tub seeing for the first time her inside fingertips;
like looking up through long wavery stalks of kelp to floating ukuleles;
like dreaming yourself acting in the wrong play;
like appearing accidentally in the background of a snapshot
      affixed to a page in an album opened briefly
      on a long low table in Japan;
like taking a history exam not studied for
      in a course you forgot you enrolled in;
like being one of a large group of men unknown to one another
      who spend the evening discovering that long ago
      you all shared the same girlfriend,
      now your wife;
like participating in a deprogramming session targeting cherished urban myths:
      No one really tried to dry her poodle in a microwave.
      No ingredients in shampoo, used as directed, can hurt you.
      Tampons contain neither asbestos nor dioxin.
      There are just as many kidney thieves in New Orleans
         as penis shrinkers in Dakar,
         none.

Tom Dilworth

Neither aspartame nor vasectomies cause cancer.
Sunscreen does not cause blindness (but may lead
     to masturbation).
Turning counter-clockwise 3 times with one eye shut
     while humming 'Yes Jesus Loves Me'
     does not prevent venereal disease.
Or it's like meeting the grandparents
     at the funeral of young friends.

Di Brandt

ZONE: <le Détroit>

after Stan Douglas

I

Breathing yellow air
here, at the heart of the dream
of the new world,
the bones of old horses and dead Indians
and lush virgin land, dripping with fruit
and the promise of wheat,
overlaid with glass and steel
and the dream of speed:
all these our bodies
crushed to appease
the 400 & 1 gods
of the Superhighway,
NAFTA, we worship you,
hallowed be your name,
here, where we are scattered
like dust or rain in ditches,
the ghosts of passenger pigeons
clouding the silver towered sky
the future clogged in the arteries
of the potholed city,
Tecumseh, come back to us
from your green grave,
sing us your song of bravery
on the lit bridge over the black river,
splayed with grief over the loss

Di Brandt

of its ancient rainbow coloured
fish swollen joy.
Who shall be fisher king
over this poisoned country,
whose borders have become
a mockery,
blowing the world to bits
with cars and cars and trucks and electricity and cars,
who will cover our splintered
bones with earth and blood,
who will sing us back into—

2

See how there's no one going to Windsor,
only everyone coming from?
Maybe they've been evacuated,
maybe there's nuclear war,
maybe when we get there we'll be the only ones.
See all those trucks coming toward us,
why else would there be rush hour on the 401
on a Thursday at nine o'clock in the evening?
I counted 200 trucks and 300 cars
and that's just since London.
See that strange light in the sky over Detroit,
see how dark it is over Windsor?
You know how people keep disappearing,
you know all those babies born with deformities,
you know how organ thieves follow tourists
on the highway and grab them at night
on the motel turnoffs,

Di Brandt

you know they're staging those big highway accidents
to increase the number of organ donors?
My brother knew one of the guys paid to do it,
$100,000 for twenty bodies
but only if the livers are good.
See that car that's been following us for the last hour,
see the pink glow of its headlights in the mirror?
That's how you know.
Maybe we should turn around,
maybe we should duck so they can't see us,
maybe it's too late,
maybe we're already dead,
maybe the war is over,
maybe we're the only ones alive.

3

So there I am, sniffing around
the railroad tracks
in my usual quest for a bit of wildness,
weeds, something untinkered with,
goldenrod, purple aster, burdocks,
defiant against creosote,
my prairie blood surging
in recognition and fellow feeling,
and O god, missing my dog,
and hey, what do you know,
there's treasure here
among these forgotten weeds,
so this is where they hang out,
all those women's breasts

cut off to keep our lawns green
and dandelion free,
here they are, dancing
their breastly ghost dance,
stirring up a slight wind in fact
and behaving for all the world
like dandelions in seed,
their featherwinged purple nipples
oozing sticky milk,
so what am I supposed to do,
pretend I haven't seen them
or like I don't care
about all these missing breasts,
how they just vanish
from our aching chests
and no one says a word,
and we just strap on fake ones,
and the dandelions keep dying,
and the grass on our lawns
gets greener and greener
and greener

4

This gold and red autumn heat,
this glorious tree splendour,
splayed out for sheer pleasure
over asphalt and concrete,
ribbons of dark desire
driving us madly toward death,
preverse, presiding over

Di Brandt

five o'clock traffic
like the queens on Church Street,
grand in their carstopping
high heels and blond wigs
and blue makeup, darling,
so nice to see you, and what,
dear one, exactly was the rush?
Or oceans, vast beyond ridicule
or question, and who cares if it's
much too hot for November,
isn't it gorgeous, darling,
and even here, in this
most polluted spit of land
in Canada, with its heart
attack and cancer rates,
the trees can still knock
you out with their loveliness
so you just wanna drop
everything and weep, or laugh,
or gather up the gorgeous
leaves, falling, and throw yourself
into them like a dead man,
or a kid, or dog,

          5
O the brave deeds of men
M*E*N, that is, they with phalli
dangling from their thighs,
how they dazzle me with
their daring exploits

Di Brandt

every time I cross the Detroit River
from down under, I mean,
who else could have given
themselves so grandly,
obediently, to this water god,
this fierce charlatan,
this glutton for sailors and young boys,
risking limbs and lives, wordlessly,
wrestling primordial mud,
so that we, mothers and maids,
could go shopping across the border
and save ourselves twenty minutes
coming and going, chatting about
this and that, our feet never
leaving the car, never mind
the mouth of the tunnel
is haunted by bits and fragments
of shattered bone and looking
every time like Diana's bridge
in Paris, this is really grand, isn't it,
riding our cares under the river
and coming out the other side
illegal aliens, needing passports,
and feeling like we accomplished
something, snatched from
our busy lives, just being there

Bronwen Wallace

Detours: An Anthology of Poets from Windsor & Essex County

Reclaiming the City

The sign says, *Windsor, City of Roses*,
but anyone who's lived here knows it's a city of hands
and dark metal, necessary as blood,
or the long lines of cars pumped from its factories
for the arteries of a continent.
A city of days produced on an assembly-line,
the sun an ancient star that doesn't chart things any more,
intruding on the dreams of those who churn with the effort
of learning this tighter chronology.
A city I came to by chance
the way I might meet a man at a party
and talk about anything at all,
never thinking he could change my life forever.
Which is not what I mean to say at all, of course;
a man at a party, putting this stanger in
as a mere figure of comparison
when what I need to say is, *you, you have*,
and what I want from this city now
is a sign, proof that I was a difference.

Tonight, I have dinner with Mark,
still in his apartment by the river.
More than anything, I envy his ease with the place,
love I want to call it, though he doesn't,
shrugging it off with that gesture
I've seen old men use for their wives,
as if what kept them in a marriage all their adult lives
were some paralysis they hadn't found a cure for yet.

Bronwen Wallace

He moved here in '67, just before the riots started in Detroit,
his balcony a ringside seat that summer
from which to watch the low hills of smoke
peaked occasionally by sirens or gunfire.
He kept his TV on the railing, tuning in particulars,
the recognizable curve of an arm throwing a bottle,
faces as young as his own, and the others, shielded by rifles
as the army moved in, but he turned the volume off,
he didn't want some newsman to explain things to him,
and now his stories stretch through pauses
more important than the words somehow,
like the fact that he's still sitting here,
taking it all in.

What we study tonight
is how Detroit has rebuilt itself, its skyline
dominated by RenCen, that space-age castle,
a city within a city, where tracks of light are elevators
carrying their passengers high into the night,
though in the older dark below
the planet is reclaiming its own,
block after block, as people move out to the suburbs
the grass moves back, bushes crowd from factories
and trees grow through the rooms of burnt-out houses.
In a few years, Mark says,
RenCen could be stranded in the middle of the forest,
an alien craft, with no-one to remember how it got there,
and tonight even the freighters on the river
move with more than their usual weariness
as if they've known all along

Detours: An Anthology of Poets from Windsor & Essex County

Bronwen Wallace

that their cargoes of oil or metal
are the lives of men and women, scrabbled from the earth
one way or another.

In this city where the night is always
forcing someone out of bed and into a factory,
dreams come as they will
and if I could travel far enough
I'd find our place on Wyandotte,
just as it was, and you
leaving for work at midnight
while the baby and I curled into sleep,
milky with it, still, in the morning
when you returned, your anger cold as the first light.
All those nights punched in, punched out
to a language I couldn't love you enough to learn.
Any more than you could.
Tuned to your talk of unions and shop-floor politics,
how could you see that I was turning
to another revolution, how our son
tore my days up by their roots
and handed me a life I had to grow to fit
if I wanted to survive.

Statistically, it's common enough. *Marital breakdown
due to stress.* Science leaves us no-one
to blame any more; though in that, how is it different
from politics or religion, our own smaller wisdoms,
whatever brings me back here, hating
what this city made of us and keeps on making

Bronwen Wallace

of so many others. *City of Roses*,
though what thrives here is restlessness;
where someone is always working, anything can happen.

And a night like this drives a hard bargain;
it won't let me get away with feeling sorry,
that makeshift emotion I rig up sometimes
to disguise my choices. I'm stuck with what
I can't reclaim: how I loved you
as much as I love my life without you now
or my own body, our marriage in this city
we came to by chance, rooting ourselves
in the child we made, wanting to, not thinking of the future
as he carries us into it.

Phil Hall

Detours: An Anthology of Poets from Windsor & Essex County

Windsor

They sure had it in for me—& my white bug—those little bastards

They pushed it down the alley—tore the gear shift out of the floor—I had to use a screw-driver to change gears to get to my orderly job on time (the old age home—Villa Maria—under the Ambassador Bridge) on those cold mornings

Zany Steve Dahl—on the radio from Detroit—while the windows defrosted—would be doing voices—Ali—Olive Oyl—between the songs—that late 70s mishmash

Whip It! by Devo & coming up later *The Chicken Song* by Doug & the Slugs

We were behind & above—a Laundromat—upstairs from Bron Wallace—Ron Baxter—& little Jeremy in his *Thank You Dr Lamaze* t-shirt—the four of us playing euchre Saturday nights

We were ancient history—or a new breed of citizens—even used cloth diapers—until they all vanished from the Laundromat dryer—I chased a grey van two blocks

They pushed my bug over—upside down—on its hood—in a pool of its own gasoline—you could see the front axle was rusted right through—the radio blaring—the wheels spinning—my landlord screaming Italian at me

Then the bikers next door (who seemed decent) broke in one grim weekend—stole my dad's little German 22 in its case & all my records—I still miss *Blowin' Yr Mind* by Van Morrison—it had "TB Sheets" on it

Phil Hall

One of my final nights there—I had—Ani—her name was—over—from behind—on the orange carpeted floor of our living room—while my wife was at work at Mother's Pizza

(The waitresses had to wear these tan laced bodices & the walls of the booths were decorated with antique photos—nameless threshing crews)

My son was 2—the first *Star Wars* had just come out & because his name is D'Arcy kids called him Darthy Vader

He could climb from his crib—had heard something—was scared I guess

He was standing in the doorway—in a plastic diaper—breathing sleep-gunk & watching us make the desperate blind alien we were up to

He said—*Daddy?*

Stephen Pender

Windsoria

There are no witnesses in Windsor.
                    —John Barlow

Under this bridge,
we find fragments of a mouth:
arguing a finer exile, a list,
or the easy distance of wind:
AM ASS DOR
says the bridge;
you have done well,
I have listened to you swim.

DOR BRIDGE
in read, inread, in red,
without witnesses, suspension
in suspension, implexure
without content, the wind
allows it seasons
and saltant bridges.

How much is and what
becomes of things extended
as if the bridge was ensouled
and we were merely waiting.

AMBASS OR BRID
now they carry guns, or wish to,
when they trim the border;

Stephen Pender

now they abjure bridges, or wish to
when the monies are sorted:
BASSA R B
full of circumstance
nothing outlives creosote,
nothing lasts long here: just
a moment, a bridge.

John Ditsky

Detours: An Anthology of Poets from Windsor & Essex County

At a Market in Detroit

What are we looking for in here today,
among the people talking in a tongue
we can't begin to cope with? And why

are we wandering among the open olive
casks—so many kinds!—or these
of peppers? These metal cans of oil

and oiled fish that fill the shelves
around us tell us nothing, beyond
a fable of far places. These stone-

shaped breads contain no messages.
Why does the eye linger on the chunk
of white cheese crumbling on a slab

of wood, the knife nearby? We like
our olives jarred, our cheese in plastic
wrap. What are we waiting to hear?

Our houses are outside, among the killers
and hors d'oeuvres. Still we listen,
as if for a signal of struck strings.

Darryl Whetter

Water Or Air

after Susan Holbrook

sure the amphibians, those bisexuals,
can do water or air
but most of us
turn corners, take one road
or another, fork our way
through the binaries

you do your own taxes or
send them to the cleaners

you put the toilet seat back down or
What's wrong with America?

you're monogamous
or mostly

you stop at one
bottle of wine

you read what amazes you or
The Stone Angel
The Book of Negroes

you vote
or let them win

Darryl Whetter

you have been changed by art
or think it a con
(though not Hollywood, never the Bible)

fiction or non

you donate to charity or
fucking taxes

you're blessed with health
or had no idea
this could still be living

latex or the pill,
pay now or pay later

you reduce, reuse and only then recycle or
Hey, me

you have kids
or have seen the writing
on Malthus's wall

gustave morin

Translation

Joyce Carol Oates

Contrary Motions

you are the rising
the pump handle flung up
like a male shriek

I am the sinking
the draining of dark water
back to the private well

your eye in its solid liquid
moves in the socket
sure as grease

icy winds
cascade along the fish-strewn shore
of Lake Erie: ice like teeth

pellets of ice loosed and biting
teeth melting back to droplets
of harmless saliva

the edge of the ice retreats
to shore   on the break-water
the water-line drops

the empty forms of winter
smudged as thumbprints
fill in again heavily with life

Jenny Sampirisi

Frogirl

(*Steps out of the assembly. Clears her throat for an extended period*)

How's our time? I don't want to go on too long. I hear: Get off already. I hear: Shut up. How are we doing? I don't want bodies shifting in seats. Feel the longness of voice. I suck space. Gill it. I feel time, up here, when I form letters. How are we doing? This pose I hold. I can't stop thinking of the electric hum between my legs. How like a tongue it is. So think this instead:

Thank god our flight was on time. My son was fussing over the chairs in the lobby. I thought what is the point? I asked him, What kind of fabric is it exactly? The fabric is itchy or causes itching. This was my son's preoccupation. His fingers were scratching the lobby chair as though it were the thing that itched.

The sound of planes are voices. We couldn't hear each other in the night. Our genitals confused one cell for another. Frog-cum-girl-cum-multiplimbed so wide open we survive.

(FROGIRL *clears her throat again as if to say more.*)

The Ns

Step back. (*Frogirl freezes in place.*) Come on. One leg then the other. Then the other. Come on. One leg. Then the other. Step back! (*Frogirl doesn't move*).

Yes, we are all here, collecting data, counting limbs, et cetera. And 'you' are the thing making noise. That is your voice in a pot bubbling. I am saying so now. Not sounding except in my throat. The sound of thinking sound. Second one and second two. Listen: in the distance I hear.

A vigilant croaking in the night to inform the others you exist. You are here and it's a sound. (*Frogirl opens her mouth and closes it over and over. Steps off stage. Now there are fewer.*)

Jenny Sampirisi

Detours: An Anthology of Poets from Windsor & Essex County

Frogirls

Dear lovely legs dear love my legs in this better pond we are coming together my fingers in our genitals in a swamp we're coming together your hands with fingers splintering in our genitals in this pond with chemicals so close to a way in a way in a way to weather the holes tic tic tic oh that's such a cliché together is so hermaphroditic tic tic tic but this is the frog frog female female all that mal in us in our best pond are you singing now can we find each other over a ruckus of planes a dread taint through this swamp who are you to come traipsing through our fucking our lovely love we've birthed without you and now you build a home here with soil cooroak coo-roak coo-roak we're trying to understand this 'you' we've made out of the hairs that fall in the bathtub or stick to the toilet seat we tic tic tic when you flush when you push yourself down the drain your factual waste your evolutionary boundaries.

The Ns

(*Some sit. Some kneel. Some continue to stand.*)

The anxiety of listening is sometimes overwhelming. We do no thing. On TV a puppet like a frog. It sings. It habits. It things a past. Gestures. Yep yep yep yep yep yep a stage. When we was just a tadpole.

L.ve .il spill rev.lt electi.n rubber bullet ri.t gear p.nd water in a h.se. Tweet a d.g a bird a clear edge. It's n.t easy being. Fr.girl y.u're n. saint. What if sex is determined by infecti.n. A bullet p.int between fingers. d.t d.t d.t

A cartoon like a frog. Dances. Wiggles. Slaps. Flip the grenouille. For our pleasure. Frog in formalwear sings if you refuse me. This happens. This happens. xx xy xo. It's all there.

Eugene McNamara

Huron Church Line

the road is in poor repair—
arrogant cars pulling boats
have a hard time of it—
the boat trailers jounce
in the ruts

the blue air shimmers
with curses and exhaust
the summer sun
through the smog
from the factories
on the river bank
is a bruise on the day

(as for boggs we knowe of nonne
in the countrie—)

the sneering   ghosts
of voyageurs
paddle through shit
dumped from cabin cruisers

YET that manie dye suddenly
by the hand of GOD
we often see it fall out so
even in this FLOURISHING &
PLENTIFUL CITIE—

Eugene McNamara

in the midst of our streets—
as for dying under hedges—
there is no hedge at all
in this countrie—

we cannot see the river
from the road
and on the river
they cannot
they cannot see
the road

I think we are lucky
not to see the river

Nasser Hussain

Detours: An Anthology of Poets from Windsor & Essex County

Everybody, now

there are 2157 people in the world, precisely
that there are others to fill six billion, is a lie
everyone is someone I met in highschool
oh I know you mister guy what cuts me off at the lights
I MET YOU BEFORE in a dream I had this morning and I thought it would be
a nice manageable world if there were only just us in it
there you are, ms I always stop in doorways
have you met mr exit blocker?
you might have interesting kids, but for the fact that he's already been born
(crap. Everything is incestuous
we pee in the same pots as our forefathers
we wii without regard to chlorofluorocarbons
where the three star wars now double
the tree kicks out its hollows and we gag being swallowed
nope, I met you before and I see you everywhere and I want to let you know
that I've whispered in your hair the secret recipe to mother's samosas the
plain truth about moses and the directions to my imaginary homeland
this poem

Robert Earl Stewart

Detours: An Anthology of Poets from Windsor & Essex County

If Not Now

There are days when I will not be satisfied with
what I've been given, and outward reality—
the dramas of the day that if collapsed would fit,
along with Manhattan, inside this box of Blue Bird
safety matches that have failed to light the barbecue again—
seems even more spacious and filled with mystery
than the most prosaic steel girder. The kind science
tells us is less not there than not not there,
like Tom Dilworth, who in a lecture on Hopkins, Pound,
or possibly Swinburne, threw himself into the lecture hall
wall in an attempt to demonstrate that one day his particles
would array themselves in just such a way as to meet up
perfectly with the spaces between the particles in the cinder
block, and he would simply vanish from sight
and come walking in the classroom door from the
hallway without. He knocked himself out cold.
That it doesn't happen every time is the reason
there's a strike zone, a ground zero, a blank page;
a guitar in the corner, coffee in a chipped porcelain cup,
insults hurled in your direction making love with
your tympanum—the reason some days are too much
with us, lashing each other with the track and field
tape measure you stole from school
trying to measure up a corner of the yard for some shade
I brought you for Mother's Day (the swirling electrons of
said structure swirling away in the grass against the
back of the house). This day, solid in its domesticity
with trips to Home Depot and Toys "R" Us, is being revealed

Robert Earl Stewart

Detours: An Anthology of Poets from Windsor & Essex County

to be much less a day than it is a dot pattern,
each dot arrayed just so—I half expect Tom Dilworth
to come tumbling from the hyacinth and tell us
to look each other in the eye, and see the darkling thrushes
of our love there, see the perverse streaks that fail us,
that prevent us from passing through the present moment
and its incumbent troubles, to see that infinitely beyond
the material, there is an intelligence that lines up matter
so we stick in place, not passing through all the time—
charging through rose bushes and coming up in a
smoked meat—that things originate out of something,
mean a lot, and proceed to exactly where
they're supposed to be.

Mary Ann Mulhern

Orphans

A widow stands beside a winter grave
her children mill like sheep
in the silent freeze of fear
their father sinking into darkness
their lives buried with him
slow starve of poverty
slaves on summer farms
searching soil and sky for their father
his love like silk on corn
his spirit rising up to feed them

Len Gasparini

Endangered Species

for Patrick Lane

In a country that was founded
on the backs of fur-bearing animals
I once saw a stuffed adult cougar
at a trade show in Vancouver's BC Place.
If there is reincarnation,
metempsychosis, transmutation, or whatever,
I hope that I come back
as a cougar, *Felis concolor*,
solitary and nocturnal in the wilds
of northern British Columbia.
I will stalk, ambush, and stab
my sharp canines into the neck
of any motherfucking nimrod
who tries to hunt me down.
I'll eat my fill; feed my kittens;
and leave the rest for the ravens.

Dorothy Mahoney

Detours: An Anthology of Poets from Windsor & Essex County

Hawk Migration

on top of the tower
we are suddenly small against the vista
of trees turning
the sun's reflection of Lake Erie and the sky
while a man defines lines with binoculars
identifies a kestrel flying low
a sharp-shinned hawk coming over the trees
another man records details

it is hawk migration at Holiday Beach
600 turkey vultures spotted
hieroglyphic sightings numbered on a board
my untrained eyes wander
to the seagulls, watch a blue jay
fly through the brush
I'm lost to this new vocabulary
of raptors and flight patterns
spotting red-tailed hawks along the 401
and being satisfied
here there is talk of Cooper's, of peregrine
like savoured names of unknown wines or words
of antiquity

Detours: An Anthology of Poets from Windsor & Essex County

Melanie Janisse

Detours: An Anthology of Poets from Windsor & Essex County

Selections from *Orioles in the Oranges*

I

There is nothing but the storm across the lake. Wind up and down in heart-beats. Watching the settling of the wake, waking the sun of this morning. The quiet of the porch, where I have sat. Listening to pain as you vanish into a creature that I pretend not to know. I sit. Facing the lake, my own refusal, hatred. The fullest of night, and I forget about candles, succumb to the darkness. As it turns out, you are just you. No knight, no prince.

The alchemy of one sleepless night. Tear-streaked, I sit deeply, finding my depths, the lake within me. It is full of awkward sinkings, borrowed ships. Old cars. Casks. Fish. Cessnas.

The morning sun is rising over the water. I decide it is better to light this candle than to curse my darkness.

I am damaged enough to be wise.

II

An unforgiving wave is washing over me. You are gone from me in fits and starts. Leaving is a tightrope of events that comb their way through everything. Even on the ferry over, were you already gone? Were you even here in the first place? You sleep away your tempers like tonic.

Melanie Janisse

I sink you to the bottom of me. Stones. The greatest of insults is that I was never enough compared to the thunder in your mind. My folly: that I thought I was.

III

My mind cleaves to this island that is me. On this island there are drug dealers and cocaine. Moth men. Burial grounds that house the bones of my ancestors. Moats and lakes and strange peeling trees. Arbutus. Birch. On this island are the old ways of judging churchgoers, stipulations. Aging beauty queens with litres of white wine and chipmunks to feed. Peanuts. Apples. Trapped in caftans and Frank Lloyd Wright houses with gossamer webs strung through, powerful and binding. Nectars. Hummingbirds and oranges sliced, and filled with grape preserves to lure the orioles closer. Taught by heart-broken ladies. There are litanies of lovers on my island. Perfect and broken. Hunters in traditional skins. A series of Wampum. Beads and nails. Pelts. Fried wild turkey nuggets in the restaurants. Good egg breakfasts. Eagles. Mountians. Cedar trees and longhouses.

Melanie Janisse

IV

There are ghosts of sad girls roaming around in nightgowns and furs. Old women with stories rimming their eyes. Bird walks. Poets live on my island. There are old clapboard homes painted white and pink. Cruising bikes and drunken drivers. There is everything in its roundness. Babies and old tractors. Witches and those who consider words like heresy while canning preserves, tilling the soil. Gentle men guarding the shipwrecks and artifacts. Flies on screens, birds that are both worshipped and slaughtered. Barns and bowling alleys from old times, full of bumblebees and swallows. Tattoos of eagles. Ball caps. Bingos. I could go on. Take you around the edges of here. Run my finger around the line of a tea saucer. Let you see. But this is my island now. I could only show you the outline of it. Like a colouring book with only the imagination left to fill in.

On my island there is you. Now dead to me. A flicker behind my eyes. A beacon of my wisdom. A lighthouse.

Robert Earl Stewart

He Disavows His Original Coyote Population Estimate

The county forester rises from his desk,
stands in his office door, listening
to the darkened nature centre,

its glass display cases of taxidermied foxes,
and the muted light of the terrariums
of fox snakes and star-nosed moles.

He calls out a name I can't make out,
then waits for a reply
before returning to his creaky chair

and our phone conversation.
He knows it's too quiet in the woods for a full moon.
He's been asked to make a retraction:

Did I say there *is* ten thousand?
The woodlots would have to be more spacious on the inside
than they are without,

like a house of leaves.
What I meant to say is there *isn't* ten thousand.
We have been shorted ten thousand.

The matter of that many coyotes
has been removed from our woodlots
by a Yahweh-like figure—

as cold and blank as the face of the sea-pocked moon.
And of what remains, I have little to say
to the positive:

They are cunning, elusive.
There could be one under your desk right now.
They can sneak in with your groceries. Watch for their eyes

peering over the jagged edge of the bag.
Listen for them snuffling for crumbs in the carpet
when you leave the room.

There are only two other possibilities, I say.
One, the investigating officer says someone turned up
in the emergency room with a bite wound on his hand—

The naturalist cannot speculate on the affairs
of men, he says. *He can as little divine from their flesh*
as he can direct the moon to wane.

He is not an alienist for the depths of men's hearts.
Off in the distance, a fox snake
unhinges its jaw.

Eugene McNamara

The Peace I Spoke Of

Meadowlarks in a stand of ash trees
birch saplings cut across dark pine

There is peace in all this

A raven's sundown shriek cuts

Deep like the plucked string
at the end of *The Cherry Orchard*

After everyone has left

Only the old servant dozing alone

Nothing stays the same

Someone near the lake shouts
I'm telling you for the last time

That peace I spoke of

Precious as something fragile
carried from one room to another

And not let fall

gustave morin

Vortext

```
══════════════════════ vortext ══════════════════════
zzzzzzzzzzzzzzzzzzzzzzzzzzzzzzzzzzzzzzzzzzzzzzzzzzzzz
zyyyyyyyyyyyyyyyyyyyyyyyyyyyyyyyyyyyyyyyyyyyyyyyyyyyz
zyxxxxxxxxxxxxxxxxxxxxxxxxxxxxxxxxxxxxxxxxxxxxxxxxyz
zyxwwwwwwwwwwwwwwwwwwwwwwwwwwwwwwwwwwwwwwwwwwwwwxyz
zyxwvvvvvvvvvvvvvvvvvvvvvvvvvvvvvvvvvvvvvvvvvvwxyz
zyxwvuuuuuuuuuuuuuuuuuuuuuuuuuuuuuuuuuuuuuuuvwxyz
zyxwvuttttttttttttttttttttttttttttttttttttttuvwxyz
zyxwvutsssssssssssssssssssssssssssssssssssstuvwxyz
zyxwvutsrrrrrrrrrrrrrrrrrrrrrrrrrrrrrrrrrrrstuvwxyz
zyxwvutsrqqqqqqqqqqqqqqqqqqqqqqqqqqqqqqqqqrstuvwxyz
zyxwvutsrqppppppppppppppppppppppppppppppppqrstuvwxyz
zyxwvutsrqpoooooooooooooooooooooooooooooopqrstuvwxyz
zyxwvutsrqponnnnnnnnnnnnnnnnnnnnnnnnnnnnopqrstuvwxyz
zyxwvutsrqponmmmmmmmmmmmmmmmmmmmmmmmmmnopqrstuvwxyz
zyxwvutsrqponmlllllllllllllllllllllllmnopqrstuvwxyz
zyxwvutsrqponmlkkkkkkkkkkkkkkkkkkkklmnopqrstuvwxyz
zyxwvutsrqponmlkjjjjjjjjjjjjjjjjjjjklmnopqrstuvwxyz
zyxwvutsrqponmlkjiiiiiiiiiiiiiiiiijklmnopqrstuvwxyz
zyxwvutsrqponmlkjihhhhhhhhhhhhhhhijklmnopqrstuvwxyz
zyxwvutsrqponmlkjihgggggggggggghijklmnopqrstuvwxyz
zyxwvutsrqponmlkjihgffffffffffffghijklmnopqrstuvwxyz
zyxwvutsrqponmlkjihgfeeeeeeeeeefghijklmnopqrstuvwxyz
zyxwvutsrqponmlkjihgfeddddddddefghijklmnopqrstuvwxyz
zyxwvutsrqponmlkjihgfedcccccdefghijklmnopqrstuvwxyz
zyxwvutsrqponmlkjihgfedcbbbcdefghijklmnopqrstuvwxyz
zyxwvutsrqponmlkjihgfedcbabcdefghijklmnopqrstuvwxyz
zyxwvutsrqponmlkjihgfedcbbbcdefghijklmnopqrstuvwxyz
zyxwvutsrqponmlkjihgfedcccccdefghijklmnopqrstuvwxyz
zyxwvutsrqponmlkjihgfeddddddddefghijklmnopqrstuvwxyz
zyxwvutsrqponmlkjihgfeeeeeeeeeefghijklmnopqrstuvwxyz
zyxwvutsrqponmlkjihgffffffffffffghijklmnopqrstuvwxyz
zyxwvutsrqponmlkjihggggggggggggghijklmnopqrstuvwxyz
zyxwvutsrqponmlkjihhhhhhhhhhhhhhhijklmnopqrstuvwxyz
zyxwvutsrqponmlkjiiiiiiiiiiiiiiiiijklmnopqrstuvwxyz
zyxwvutsrqponmlkjjjjjjjjjjjjjjjjjjjklmnopqrstuvwxyz
zyxwvutsrqponmlkkkkkkkkkkkkkkkkkkkklmnopqrstuvwxyz
zyxwvutsrqponmlllllllllllllllllllllllmnopqrstuvwxyz
zyxwvutsrqponmmmmmmmmmmmmmmmmmmmmmmmmmnopqrstuvwxyz
zyxwvutsrqponnnnnnnnnnnnnnnnnnnnnnnnnnnnopqrstuvwxyz
zyxwvutsrqpoooooooooooooooooooooooooooooopqrstuvwxyz
zyxwvutsrqppppppppppppppppppppppppppppppppqrstuvwxyz
zyxwvutsrqqqqqqqqqqqqqqqqqqqqqqqqqqqqqqqqqrstuvwxyz
zyxwvutsrrrrrrrrrrrrrrrrrrrrrrrrrrrrrrrrrrrstuvwxyz
zyxwvutsssssssssssssssssssssssssssssssssssstuvwxyz
zyxwvuttttttttttttttttttttttttttttttttttttttuvwxyz
zyxwvuuuuuuuuuuuuuuuuuuuuuuuuuuuuuuuuuuuuuuuvwxyz
zyxwvvvvvvvvvvvvvvvvvvvvvvvvvvvvvvvvvvvvvvvvvvwxyz
zyxwwwwwwwwwwwwwwwwwwwwwwwwwwwwwwwwwwwwwwwwwwwwxyz
zyxxxxxxxxxxxxxxxxxxxxxxxxxxxxxxxxxxxxxxxxxxxxxxxxyz
zyyyyyyyyyyyyyyyyyyyyyyyyyyyyyyyyyyyyyyyyyyyyyyyyyyyz
zzzzzzzzzzzzzzzzzzzzzzzzzzzzzzzzzzzzzzzzzzzzzzzzzzzz
```

swers

that's a toad
that's not a toad
that's a tree
that's a mushroom
that's a bird
that's a rock
that's water
that's land
that's sun
that's more water, deep and fast
that's not a noise you need to worry about
that one is
that's flat
that's got a dip in it
that's sharp
those are soft if you pile them up
that's a bear shit
that's a fox
that's too far
we want to be closer
there's a name for that, but I can't recall
there's a name for that and I don't care
that's enough
that's a tree a rock a lake a star a fire and a meal
oh that's it

Laurie Smith

on tracing the pedigree for best in show

time searching,
looking for continuity,
the key to perfection,
the big gamble,
incestuous possibilities
buried like puzzles
in breeding lines, in names
that might boast
some string of purity

i am
up to my double helix in
layers
of paper
trails with
no tails, unless

you want to really go back,
but soon you run out
of reliable sources,
depend on carbon dated info
maybe hearsay,
'til the language inconsistencies
and glyphs
add to the mix

then someone helpful surely
thumps a bible, tells you
darwin lied the answer's here:
and two by two they did board the ark,
with men and monkeys

Dorothy Mahoney

Bequest

wishing for transplanted summers of thick leaves
and dark raspberries of my grandmother's farm
we dug deeply into her rich soil knowing
she would have told us to take
the raspberry canes, roots severed
where we walked the tops of the last furrow
into the weeds along the greenhouse, hearing
the hard anger of a yellow jacket
seeking a broken pane's escape

running down the field, our black patent shoes dusty
as greenhouse glass, our lips and fingers red
pointing at a feather or fallen egg
far from the orchard where beetles dug
deeper into a headless sparrow
while grandmother's cat weaved between us
as we wandered through rusted hollyhocks
seeing my grandmother, her white hair caught
like the last glimpse of a cottontail
disappearing into brambles
we searched the yard of our summers
pigeons scared into flight
flapping in wide circles
returning and returning

resisting pints of raspberries sold in cellophane
we stand over barren canes in city plots

John Ditsky

Buds

My little girl
takes cheese, sections of sweet
peaches, all on the point of a sharp
knife up to her young mouth;
we, sitting in deck chairs
out in the lakeside sun,
we see only the knife
point and   *Ahhh!*   our learned
fears in an intake of breath.

My little girl
does not note our astonishment;
content within her browning skin,
she savors flavor that experience
preserves us from. The blade
pays homage to her blood, defers
to self-assurance rich as wine
in her new veins. Life
runs in excess down her chin.

Dani Couture

Dead Letters

For John Ditsky

Your cupboards filled with Italy and Alaska,
bathtub overflowing with South America.

On the back of each postcard my tiny scrawl,
like electric blue wire, links village to village.

I imagine your house pillared
with bundles of glossy destinations.

Foreign anecdotes fill your breadbox,
the corners of Talkeetna and Temagami peek

from beneath your welcome mat. If only
I had afforded you the opportunity

to write back, you could have told me
you'd already left, packed your leather bags

for good, and gone.

Hips

Like the curve
of a hockey stick
the soft bend in the road
at dusk, the way
a branch bows
with the full weight
of apples in the fall
I saw curves
everywhere—
I thought of all
the young girls whose
figures would blossom
with my adolescent
fantasies, their hips
swaying in the cool spring
the slope of the jeans
or the gingham dress
the way they moved
with unctuous grace
When I was 12
the deciding factor
my buddy told me
was a good set of hips
—the pick of a good
wife lay with the hips
perfect for childbearing
and we'd stand
on the street

Detours: An Anthology of Poets from Windsor & Essex County

at the Parkview Diner
and take inventory
of the young moms
size up their hips
cock our heads
to one side
and nod in agreement
over the perfect set—
one as slender and lithe
as a balsam tree, others
as wide and proud
as the bumper
of a Chev Impala
I had become
sexually aware at 12
silently measuring
the half-moon like
curves as they sauntered
down aisles, as they moved
between tables in the
school cafeteria
I saw curves
everywhere—
catching the Yankee
Billy Martin sliding
to one side to make
a play at second
his hips in the October

series like the elegance
of a cougar moving
to snare his prey
I saw hospital
pinstripers pouring
out at the end of a day
their lovely bodies
as smooth as a warm
current in the lake
I saw Elvis bump
and grind, his white
suedes flashing on
a darkly-lit stage
hips swiveling
like a well-oiled
engine
I saw curves
everywhere—
I didn't see breasts
I didn't fixate
on crotches
or the slope of
a neckline
or the nakedness
of thighs
I saw hips
I saw hips
I saw hips

Foamula

Foams forms
Forms foam
Form foams
Foam foams
Foams, foams forms
The foamillac of foams
Forms foam
Blanks by foamage
By the foam of
Form, form foams
Old man foamer
Foamotic foamiletics foam
Foams, hello
Foam
Afoam for foam
Foamin' A (foamen!)
Gulf foamen
Poluphloisboios foambé
With foam
Foamicidal
Foamiacs
Giving foam this
It's foam alright
Avian foam
Natural foam
Evian foam
Leaving foam going
Going, going foam

Louis Cabri

Foameme's foamk that

Foam key city

Foamdsor's

Infoamation of the foam

Is to infoam you

O foameo, stack

Foam in peace or not

At foam saws

(Honk for foam)

Saw foam

Saws foam

So in foam

On the word foam (on the word foam)

Foamings for dollars

Foamed the foam (and the foam foamed)

I am foamerican

Foamterfeit

Foamy

Foam me

Foam me!

My foamies

Foamonal

Have you haagen foam

Hog foam

Today in foamlish

Height as the foamans

Do gulfs foam

Foamings for lollards, mallards

Foamen two

Nobody's foam

Foamers fee

Foam fum

Foambled

Foam luck

Foaming right

Foaming rights

Foamologo

Centric foamo

Foams to pace

Foam to space

The Foam

Face the foam

Foamous foam

Foam-a-long foamathon

Merrygo foamerie

Foamers foamily

Foamerid

Dolly the foam

Foam-out

Foam and out

Foo foam

Form foams

Forms foam

Foams forms

Foams, foams

Foam, foams

Kate Hargreaves

Ribfest

Her ribs snap. Her ribs tickle. Her ribs protrude approximately the same distance as her breasts when her push-up bra is in the wash. Her underwire sticks her in the ribs. Her ribs bruise and swell. Her ribs taste better sans barbecue sauce or Tabasco. Her top right rib broke in a slip'n slide accident when she was nine and healed on its own leaving a large deposit of bone jutting out of her chest that makes wearing a bikini top in public lopsided. Her collarbones. Her sternum. Her rack. Her ribbed for her pleasure. Her vote for your favourite rib recipe from our forty-two vendors this weekend only at. Her stick to your ribs. Her ribs stick. Her ribs clatter against one another inside her chest. Her ribs pierce her lungs every time she quickens to a jog. Her spare tire. Her spare ribs. Her spare hips. Her spare vertebrae. Her ribs spent all day Sunday in bed while she cleaned out the crawlspace. Her ribs cage. Her ribs leak marinade all over the wool. Her ribs collapse under the boning. Her. Rib. I. She prefers ribs with a little less meat on the bone. Her ribs don't see eye to eye. Her eyes rib and slit. Her ribs took off in the middle of the night. Her ribs might come back if they smell the bowl of milk she left out on the porch. Her knit one purl two rib one.

The Delectable Trip

One year we ate our way
across northern Ontario.
Mile high lemon pie in Wawa
tart on the tongue, sweet
in the memory, perfect
poached eggs in Agawa Canyon
in a café with "puppies for sale"
that tumbled by the doorstep.
The yellow yolks were soft
and soaked into the toast.
The whites didn't run!
Dune Lake was Paddy's Place,
boasting chopped root vegetables
in savoury broth. Their ladies'
room was sponge-painted pink
traced with climbing morning
glories. St Ignace's thick slices
of blueberry pie dripped with juice, purpling
the lips, silvery galvanized gathering pail
waiting by the kitchen door.
Coleman hosted the world's best Denver sandwich.
A flock of speckled hens scratched and clucked
in the yard outside the restaurant window.
And I guess we saw tumbling waterfalls and silver mines.

Emily Schultz

Pencils Down

The city is half-erased by fog, and you walk along
with dream slowness until you're told: pencils down.

Your dad drives you in a car gone four cars ago—
now a hull, or crushed, or rebuilt and resold. Pencils down.

In a city that is four cities ago, a hull of a city, a crushed city,
a sold-for-scrap city—though April is its own city. Pencils down.

The afternoon is thick as bathwater, cool. The sky milky and round
as chrysanthemum. The lead-scent threat of rain, like pencils set down.

Your uncle smells like your father when you embrace at the airport:
cigarettes, Certs. Lost uncle, gone uncle. Another city. Pencils down.

Your half-erased cousin walks through trees in a park you've never seen
to meet your uncle in a fog of green and shake hands. Pencils down.

Your brother sings for God, though the song is Elvis's. The bricks
of this town the colour of mortar. Lawns hold up the jockeys. Pencils down.

The amateur warble of trumpet in a basement apartment, three cities ago,
trembles, tumbles through the vacant city that is, that isn't

a hull around you. Though the city is silent, it's dense as sound.
In the fog you turn, and turn, and turn. Pencils down.

John Ditsky

Clout

When the rookies of your youth
retire, & the remembered stars
of back-then are all Hall-
of-Famed & harmless: ink
in the record books: cards
in a pack, rubber-banded,
in the back of a desk drawer,
then yours is new knowledge

of oldness. Though your body
turns up at the training
camp, jogging in place
& chasing the flies of necessity,
your mind has not made
the cut: already, it begs
a job scouting the bushes,
tentative as mud on cleats.

Joyce Carol Oates

The Secret of the Water Off Point Pelee

Ohio's shore is out of sight today and
the lake is therefore infinite.
We are standing cold in the waves
staring at the waves breaking
about our soft stomachs.
What is this din in the air?

Fish are flopping onto the hot sand
whitely like rubber fish. We are
swimming in white foam. We are
rocked by the happy spasms of
our bodies' muscles. What a cataclysm
of seagulls and fish and human
arms and heads!

In this infinite lake you encircle me
with your arms loving like the water,
intimate down to the pores
of your skin. I see the crease of untanned flesh
at your throat—with your cold lips you suck
these old, old freckles on my shoulder.
The waves knock us apart.

Joyce Carol Oates

Detours: An Anthology of Poets from Windsor & Essex County

We struggle back together again.
We collide. Our lungs are pumping like
arms and legs—we will stay afloat!
nostrils clean and clear of this water!
Very cold is the side of your face, my love,
your loving skull.
The air gasps around us.

Waves fight and ebb and fight again.
There are shouts of children and airplanes
in another windy element
and waves and our pumping lungs that celebrate
what is left of us—alive, in love, in this
crashing water off Point Pelee—
We have not gone down today.

Tom Dilworth

How are You?

I always answer with
a polite, irksome (for me), lie.
I want a new reply.

Phlegmatic or Sanguine,
      whose meanings I forget,
or Insouciant (ditto),
      to use when feeling elusive,
Feckless,
Soporific,
Quotidian,
Drunk, Fluthered, Plastered, Screwed, Tight, Blotto, Sozzled, Well-oiled,
Fluthery-eyed, Cock-eyed, Blind, Pie-eyed—take your pick.
Or
Compared to what? or Ask yo mama,
but one word's easier.

Flatulent,
Aroused,
Lugubrious,
Pilpulistic,
Rebarbative,
Dying, (Egypt, dying),
Louche,
Infra dig,
Most of the above covered by
Postlapsarian.

Tom Dilworth

Still, after amassing so much ammunition,
when ambushed by the question,
I always merely answer, 'Fine'.
(No point adding 25¢,
few would get it.)

Some I know answer, 'Never better.'
Eventually, I'm glad to report,
they explode.

Dani Couture

lessons learned in the county

you can skin a cat the same way you would a rabbit, if you wanted to.

don't touch the barrel of a rifle: you'll leave prints that will ruin the finish.

always listen for trains.

check your snares often: a dead animal scares off live ones.

never register all of your guns.

always wear layers.

know what's in season and where to find it.

never point a gun, unless you're intending to shoot.

make sure you know a good butcher who'll work at night.

never shoot from the car.

bring extra socks.

Phil Hall

Adios Polka

Whenever I get lost
Ontario does not wound me

the mewl & skitter of the half-eyes at the registries

have defined distance as health—& nostalgia
as a gossamer sac writhing with tent-worms

(flutter-smeared & eaten green the wild grapes)

these slips booklet-stipends collectible-spills curios
I balance a fortress of / if I must be home / *be hame*

are apolitical except in their endurance

it has rained 3 days & these pioneer logs are sponges
maps out-of-date unhinged on the pine floor

(wide first-growth planed buttery / *laned uttery*)

there is nowhere to go off
but wordward

Permissions

Grateful acknowledgement is made for permission to reprint work by the following presses and poets:

SALVATORE ALA: "Unloading Watermelons at the Windsor Market" and "Visions of a Country Road" are reprinted from *Straight Razor and Other Poems* (2004) by permission of Biblioasis.

DI BRANDT: "Zone" is reprinted from *Now You Care* (2003) by permission of Coach House Press.

LOUIS CABRI: "Foamula" is reprinted from *Poetryworld* (2010) by permission of Capilano University Editions.

DANI COUTURE: "midnight grocery shopping after watching days and days of viking week on the history channel" and "lessons learned in the county" are reprinted from *Good Meat* (2006), and "Dead Letter" is reprinted from *Sweet* (2010) by permission of Pedlar Press.

JOHN DITSKY: "Buds" first appeared in *Scar Tissue* (1978) by Vesta Publications, and "At a Market in Detroit" first appeared in *Friend & Lover* (1981) by The Ontario Press, reprinted by permission of the author's estate.

MARTY GERVAIS: "The Cow on the Bardstown Road", "Hips", "The Kid" are reprinted from *to be now: new and selected poems 1989-2003* (2003) by permission of Mosaic Press.

PHIL HALL: "Windsor" is reprinted from *The Little Seamstress* (2010) by permission from Pedlar Press. "Adios Polka" is reprinted from *Killdeer* (2011), and "Ruthlessly Local" is reprinted from *White Porcupine* (2007) by permission of BookThug.

MELANIE JANISSE: selections, pages 60-63, are reprinted from *Orioles in the Oranges* (2009) by permission of Guernica Editions.

DOROTHY MAHONEY: "Bequest", "Hawk Migration", and "LaSalle Woodlot" are reprinted from *Returning to the point* (2001) by permission of Black Moss Press.

NICOLE MARKOTIĆ: "The mask off, but the mitts on:" and "sons and nets" are reprinted from *Bent at the Spine* (2012) by permission of BookThug.

EUGENE MCNAMARA: "Punching In" first appeared in *Call It a Day* (1984) by blewointmentpress, and "Huron Church Line" first appeared in *Diving For the Body* (1974) by Borealis Press, reprinted by permission of the author. "That Peace I Spoke Of" is reprinted from *Dreaming of Lost America* (2012) by permission of Guernica Editions.

GUSTAVE MORIN: "train track" first appeared in *Sun Kissed Oranges* by Sergio Forest /gustave morin (1995) by Scratch n Sniff press, reprinted with permission of the author. "translation" first appeared in *The Windsor Salt* (1998) by Common Ground Editions, further collected in *A Penny Dreadful* (2003) by Insomniac Press, and now carried by *Spaghetti Dreadful* (2004) by Ubuweb, reprinted by permission of the author.

MARY ANN MULHERN: "Orphans" and "censored" are reprinted from *The Red Dress* (2003) by permission of Black Moss Press.

JOYCE CAROL OATES: "Love and Its Derangements" and "The Secret of the Water Off Point Pelee" from *Love and Its Derangements* (1970), and "Contrary Motions" by Joyce Carol Oates is reprinted from *Angel Fire* (1973) by permission of Ontario Review Inc.

JENNY SAMPIRISI: selections, pages 84-87, are reprinted from *Croak* (2011) by permission of Coach House Press.

EMILY SCHULTZ: "The Thing Defines Itself" is reprinted from *Songs for the Dancing Chicken* (2007) by permission of ECW.

PETER STEVENS: "To Each his own Ann Landers" first appeared in F*amily Feelings & Other Poems* (1974) by Alive Press, reprinted by permission of the author's estate. "Through Put" is reprinted from *Swimming in the Afternoon* (2003) by permission of Black Moss Press.

ROBERT EARL STEWART: "Field Notes Towards a Deeper Understanding" and "If Not Now" are reprinted from *Something Burned Along the Southern Border* (2009), and "He Disavows His Original Coyote Population Estimate" is reprinted from *Campfire Radio Rhapsody* (2011) by permission of Mansfield Press.

BRONWEN WALLACE: "Reclaiming the City" and "Lonely for the Country" are re-printed from *Common Magic* (1985) by permission of Oberon Press.

DARRYL WHETTER: "Sex: The Selfish Gene, the XX and a Bottle of Shiraz" , "Country Dog" and "Water Or Air" are reprinted from *Origins* (2012) by permission of Palimpsest Press.

Photography Acknowledgements

PAGE 19: "Men at Work" by Dawn Marie Kresan. Photograph taken on Main Street in Kingsville.

PAGE 22: "Children at Play" by Robert Earl Stewart. Photograph taken while looking East down Baseline Road in Lakeshore.

PAGE 30: "Wine Route Ahead" by Dawn Marie Kresan. Photograph taken on Division Road in Kingsville.

PAGE 40: "Curve Ahead" by Robert Earl Stewart. Photograph taken at Walker Road, just off the 401 in Windsor.

PAGE 48: "Do Not Enter" by Robert Earl Stewart. Photograph taken where Ontario Street becomes Giles Boulevard in Windsor.

PAGE 50: "Information Booth" by Susan Holbrook. Photograph taken inside Point Pelee National Park.

PAGE 56: "Slow Moving Vehicle" by Aimee Parent. Photograph taken on a farm near McGregor.

PAGE 64: "Hazard" by Robert Earl Stewart. Photograph taken while looking west on Country Road #42 in Tecumseh.

PAGE 71: "To the Ambassador Bridge" by Aimee Parent. Photograph taken on Cabana Road in Windsor.

PAGE 81: "Two Way Traffic" by Aimee Parent. Photograph taken on Highway #3, near Essex.

PAGE 91: "Hidden Intersection" by Robert Earl Stewart. Photograph taken while looking southwest across the fields along Manning Road in Tecumseh.

PAGE 101: "To Jack Miner Bird Sanctuary" by Dawn Marie Kresan. Photograph taken on the corner of Division and Road #3 in Kingsville.

PAGE 105: "Viewing Area" by Susan Holbrook. Photograph taken inside Point Pelee National Park.

PAGE 116: "Roundabout" by Robert Earl Stewart. Photograph taken on Erie Street at Langlois Avenue in Windsor.

PAGE 128: "Dangerous Currents" by Susan Holbrook. Photograph taken near the tip at Point Pelee National Park.

PAGE 125: "Must Turn" by Robert Earl Stewart. Photograph taken looking west across Manning Road, at the border of Tecumseh and Lakeshore.

PAGE 131: "Detour" by Robert Earl Stewart. Photograph taken along Provincial Road, West of Walker in Windsor.

Editor Biographies

SUSAN HOLBROOK teaches North American Literatures and Creative Writing at the University of Windsor, and is the current poetry editor for *The Windsor Review*. Her poetry books include the Trillium-nominated *Joy Is So Exhausting* (2009), the chapbook *Good Egg Bad Seed* (2004), and *misled* (1999), which was shortlisted for the Pat Lowther Memorial Award and the Stephan G. Stephansson Award. She recently co-edited *The Letters of Gertrude Stein and Virgil Thomson: Composition as Conversation* (2010). Holbrook has lived in California, Venezuela, B.C., Alberta, Spain, Abu Dhabi, and Tuscaloosa, Alabama, but finally found paradise when she moved to Point Pelee in 2002.

DAWN MARIE KRESAN received her Honours BA in English Literature and MA in Literature and Cultural Studies from the University of Windsor. She also has an advanced certificate in graphic design with a print concentration through Sessions College for Professional Design, and has studied a variety of creative interests including bookbinding, stained glass art, and letterpress printing. Her poetry books include *Muse* (2013) and a limited edition chapbook *Framed* (2009). She grew up in Amherstburg, detasseling corn each summer, then moved to Windsor for university, working weekends and summers at the Chrysler auto factory. She currently lives in Kingsville, where she works as a freelance graphic designer and the publisher of Palimpsest Press. Kresan has been involved in many local literary activities, including being a founding member of Literary Arts Windsor, a past committee member of Bookfest Windsor, and recently Palimpsest helped sponsor writing workshops in Kingsville.

Author Biographies

SALVATORE ALA was born and still resides in Windsor. He's published three books of poetry: *Clay of the Maker* (1998); *Straight Razor and Other Poems* (2004); and most recently, *Lost Luggage* (2011). He has also published six broadsides of poetry. His poems have appeared in numerous journals and anthologies.

DI BRANDT has published more than a dozen books of poetry, fiction, creative essays and literary criticism, including *questions i asked my mother* (1987), *Agnes in the sky* (1990), *Jerusalem, beloved* (1995), and *Now You Care* (2003). She has been nominated for or won many awards, including The Gerald Lampert Award, CAA National Poetry Prize, Griffin Prize, Trillium Ontario Book Award, and the Pat Lowther Award. She taught English and Creative Writing at the University of Windsor from 1996 to 2005. "Zone poems" were commissioned by the Art Gallery of Windsor as part of the Stan Douglas exhibition "Le Detroit," and were later performed with the Windsor Symphony Orchestra.

LOUIS CABRI came to Windsor in 2005 and teaches poetry and theory at the University of Windsor. His books include *Poetryworld* (2010), *—that can't* (2009), and *The Mood Embosser* (2002). He has edited *The False Laws of Narrative: The Poetry of Fred Wah and PhillyTalks* and co-edited hole magazine and hole books as well as issues of Open Letter, ESC: English Studies in Canada and *The Poetic Front* (forthcoming).

DANI COUTURE is the author of *Good Meat* (2006), *Sweet* (2010), and *Algoma* (2011). *Sweet* was nominated for the Trillium Book Award for Poetry and won the ReLit Award for poetry. In 2011, Dani also received an Honour of Distinction from The Writers' Trust Dayne Ogilvie Prize. She is the literary editor at *THIS Magazine*. Couture has a long-time connection to Essex County: it's where her mother was born and raised; she lived there between the ages of 15 and 23, and attended the

University of Windsor. She returns frequently to visit her family home on the shores of the Detroit River.

TOM DILWORTH has taught English literature at the University of Windsor since 1977. He is writing the biography of the modern British painter and poet David Jones, and is the author of *Reading David Jones* (2008) and *The Shape of Meaning in the Poetry of David Jones* (1988). He edited *Jones's illustrated Rime of the Ancient Mariner* (2005), *Jones's Wedding Poems* (2002), and *Inner Necessities: the Letters of David Jones to Desmond Chute* (1984), and co-edited *The Letters of Gertrude Stein and Virgil Thomson: Composition as Conversation* (2010). His recent poetry has appeared in *The Common Sky, Notre Dame Review, Rampike, Salmagundi, Ontario Review, Poetry* (Chicago), and *Windsor Review*.

JOHN DITSKY was born in Detroit in 1938. Aside from the time of his doctoral studies at New York University, he lived, taught and wrote in the Detroit/Windsor area, serving as professor of Creative Writing and American Literature at the University of Windsor for almost four decades. He was a beloved mentor and an inspiration to hundreds of aspiring writers in the area. He published four collections of poetry, five critical volumes, and hundreds of critical articles and poems. He was poetry editor of *The Windsor Review* for many years. He died in 2006.

LEN GASPARINI was born and raised in Windsor, Ontario. He is the author of numerous books of poetry and five short story collections, including *The Snows of Yesteryear* (2011). His new collection of poetry and lyrical prose, *The Love of Women*, is forthcoming in 2014. He divides his time between Toronto and his hometown.

ALEX GAYOWSKY was born and still lives in Windsor, Ontario. She received her MA in English Literature and Creative Writing from the University of Windsor, and is currently working towards a Bachelor of Education. In her spare time, she maintains a keen interest in paper goods by participating in local artisanal craft fairs.

MARTY GERVAIS is Windsor's first poet laureate. He is also the recipient of the prestigious Toronto's Harbourfront Festival Prize (1998) for his contributions to Canadian letters, was awarded the Milton Acorn People's Poetry Award, and has won sixteen Ontario Newspaper Awards for journalism. In 2003, Gervais was given City of Windsor Mayor's Award for *To Be Now: Selected Poems.* As a writer, he has written more than a dozen books of poetry, two plays and a novel. In 2006 Gervais and his work were the subject of an award-winning Bravo Television episode of *Heart of a Poet* produced by Canadian filmmaker Maureen Judge. Gervais is the publisher of Black Moss Press, and the managing editor of *The Windsor Review.* He currently teaches at the University of Windsor.

PHIL HALL earned an Honours BA and a Masters in English and Creative Writing at the University of Windsor between 1972 and 1978. His book of essay-poems, *Killdeer*, won the 2011 Governor General's Award for poetry in English, and also the 2012 Trillium Book Award. His poetry has also been twice nominated for the Griffin Poetry Prize. He has taught writing at York University, Ryerson Polytechnical University, Seneca College, George Brown College, and elsewhere. He has been poet-in-residence at Sage Hill Writing Experience, The Pierre Berton House, & Queens University. He currently lives near Perth, Ontario.

KATE HARGREAVES slept, ate, and read for two decades in Amherstburg, before trekking to Windsor where she now lives and works in publishing. She holds an MA in English & Creative Writing from the University of Windsor, and has published in *Room, filling Station, Carousel, Drunken Boat, Descant, The Antigonish Review*, and *The Windsor ReView*'s "Best Writers Under 35" issue. She spends her spare time collecting bruises as a roller derby skater with Windsor's Border City Brawlers, and releases her first book, *Talking Derby*, in 2013.

NASSER HUSSAIN lived in Old Sandwich Town for six years. During that time, he completed a MA in English and Creative Writing at the University of Windsor, and in collaboration with Tamara Kowalska, created the reading series "Juice". Moving to the UK to complete a PHD in literature, he now teaches Literature and Creative Writing at a number of universities in Yorkshire.

MELANIE JANISSE is a native of Windsor, where she retained memories of old docks jutting out into the Detroit River and strange underground drives to her father's hometown of Detroit. She obtained degrees from Concordia University in Communication and Emily Carr in Visual Arts. Her ouevre of work includes: a book of poems, a regular literary column in Open Book Toronto/Open Book Ontario, and a nearly completed MFA from OCAD University.

LENORE LANGS has lived in Windsor all her adult life. She worked in a lab at the Detroit Institute of Cancer Research and taught creative and expository writing at the University of Windsor. She has been or is involved in Project Ploughshares, the Gaia Women of the Great Lakes Basin, Save the Children, The United Church of Canada, Raging Grannies, and various poetry groups. She is co-publisher of Cranberry Tree Press, and the chair of the planning committee for BookFest Windsor.

DOROTHY MAHONEY was born in Windsor, and is a retired English teacher with two poetry books: *Through Painted Skies* (1997) and *Returning to the Point* (2001). She is included in several anthologies by Cranberry Tree Press and Leaf Press. She is currently working on a collection of short stories.

NICOLE MARKOTIĆ is a novelist, critic, and poet. Her six books include three of poetry: *Connect the Dots* (1994), *Minotaurs & Other Alphabets* (1998), and *Bent at the Spine* (2012). She has also published two novels, an edited collection of poetry by Dennis Cooley, and a co-edited (with Sally Chivers) anthology of essays concerning representations of disability. As well, she has numerous publications in literary journals, edits the chapbook series, Wrinkle Press, and has worked as a book editor for various presses. Currently, she is Professor of English Literature, Creative Writing, and Disability Studies at the University of Windsor.

EUGENE MCNAMARA was born in Oak Park, Illinois, and moving to Windsor, Ontario in 1959, he taught at the University of Windsor until his retirement in 1995. During that time he founded the Creative Writing Program and the University of Windsor Review. Over the years, he has received many awards, including the University of Windsor Alumni Award for Distinguished Teaching and the City of Windsor's Mayor's Award for Literacy Excellence. In 2008, the Eugene McNamara Scholarship Award for Creative Writing was established at the University of Windsor. *Dreaming of Lost America* (2012) is his sixteenth collection of poems.

GUSTAVE MORIN won a poetry contest in 1989 while still in high school; he's been a peripheral fixture on Windsor's arts scene ever since. He's published many books, organized hundreds of exhibitions and events, served on the boards of local arts organizations (notably, Common Ground, 1995–present; House of Toast, 2001–present) and, under the rubric 23 Skidoo! has produced many short films with cohort Jarrod Ferris. In conjunction with his publishing, he has lectured, performed, exhibited and read his work at many venues across the continent. His work is housed in public and private collections all over the world.

MARY ANN MULHERN is a Windsor teacher, poet and former nun. She began writing poetry after attending a writing seminar at the University of Windsor, 2001. Her first collection, *The Red Dress* (2003), received national attention in a CBC interview on *Tapestry*. *Touch the Dead* (2006) and *When Angels Weep* (2008) were both short-listed for the Acorn-Plantos Award. Her fifth book, *Brides in Black* was published in 2012.

JOYCE CAROL OATES was born in Lockport, New York. She moved to Detroit in 1961, where she began teaching at the University of Detroit. Influenced by the Vietnam War and the Detroit race riots, she accepted a teaching position at the University of Windsor in 1967. Oates lived in Windsor for a decade, before moving to Princeton in 1977, where she is currently a Professor in Humanities at Princeton University. While in Windsor, Oates and her husband, Raymond J. Smith, founded a literary magazine called *The Ontario Review* in 1974, on which Oates served as associate editor. A prolific writer, Oates has written numerous novels, short stories, dramas, essays, memoirs, children's books, and poetry collections. She has either won or been nominated for several awards, including the National Book Award, National Book Critics Circle Award, O. Henry Award, and the Pulitzer Prize.

STEPHEN PENDER moved to Windsor after completing his PHD at the University of Toronto in 2000. He teaches Early Modern British Literature at the University of Windsor, and is a fellow of the Centre for Research in Reasoning, Argumentation, and Rhetoric. He has been director of the Humanities Research Group, and from 2007–2012, he held a junior research leadership chair in the Faculty of Arts and Social Sciences. In 2003, he co-edited *The Common Sky: Canadian Writers against the War in Iraq*. He very much likes stout, and recently published his first collection of poetry, *Histologies* (2007).

JENNY SAMPIRISI received both her BA and MA in English and Creative Writing at the University of Windsor. She is the author of *Croak* (2011) and *is/was* (2009). She has held positions as Managing Editor for BookThug, co-director of the Scream Literary Festival, and co-director of the Toronto New School of Writing. She is the recipient of the 2011 KM Hunter Artist Award for Literature. She teaches English literature and creative writing at Ryerson University and has helped to develop several pilot programs at the university for at risk, Aboriginal and returning student populations.

EMILY SCHULTZ grew up in Wallaceburg, Ontario. She lived in Windsor in the 1990s and received her BA in English from the University of Windsor. Her most recent novel is *The Blondes* (2012). She is co-publisher of the literary journal Joylandmagazine.com and the author of two other novels, a short story collection, and the poetry book *Songs for the Dancing Chicken* (2007). She currently divides her time between southwestern Ontario and New York.

VANESSA SHIELDS has made her home, her family and her work life flourish in Windsor. Her first book, *Laughing Through A Second Pregnancy—A Memoir*, was published in 2011. Her poetry, short stories and photography has been published in various literary magazines. She is currently editing her first Young Adult novel. She mentors, guest speaks, and teaches creative writing. She also created "Poetry On Demand", which helps make poetry fun and accessible for all.

LAURIE SMITH holds a B.ED and MA in Creative Writing from the University of Windsor. Currently working as an event planner and as a freelance editor and writing coach, she facilitates workshops, and is co-publisher of Cranberry Tree Press. Twice she won the Mayor's Award of Excellence in the Arts. Her most recent collection is *The Truth About Roller Skating* (2011).

PETER STEVENS was born in Manchester, England in 1927 and came to Canada in 1957. He moved to Windsor in 1969 to teach literature at the University of Windsor. Stevens served as a contributing editor to *The Ontario Review*, and was poetry editor of *The Canadian Forum* and *The Literary Review of Canada*. He was also founding director of Sesame Press in Windsor. His first collection of poems, *Nothing but Spoons*, was published in 1969. His most recent collection was *States of Mind* (2001). He is also the author of several plays, three of which received performances in Detroit and Windsor. A jazz connoisseur, he was a regular contributor to CBC Radio's National network jazz shows, as well as a jazz columnist for *The Windsor Star*. Stevens died in 2009.

ROBERT EARL STEWART was born in Windsor in 1974. He spent two years as a county reporter at *The Windsor Star*, and since 2005 has been the editor of *The LaSalle Post*. His first collection of poetry, *Something Burned Along the Southern Border* (2009), was shortlisted for the Gerald Lampert Memorial Award. It was followed by *Campfire Radio Rhapsody* (2011). He lives with his wife and their three children in Windsor's historic Walkerville neighbourhood.

BRONWEN WALLACE was born in Kingston, Ontario, where she attended Queen's University. In 1970, she moved to Windsor, where she founded a women's bookstore and became an activist for the feminist and working class movements. She lived in Windsor for seven years, beginning what was to become her first poetry collection, *Common Magic* (1985). In total, she wrote five poetry collections, and a book of short stories published posthumously in 1990. Wallace died of cancer in 1989. The Bronwen Wallace Award for Emerging Writers, funded by the Writers' Trust of Canada, is an annual prize given to a promising writer under the age of thirty-five, and who is unpublished in book form.

DARRYL WHETTER is the author of three novels, a short story collection, and a collection of poems, *Origins* (2012). *A Sharp Tooth in the Fur* was named to *The Globe and Mail's Top 100 Books of 2003*. He has published poems, stories, and book reviews in Canada's best journals—including *Descant*, *The Fiddlehead*, *Arc*, *The New Quarterly*, and *Prairie Fire*. Whetter has been a professor of English and Creative Writing at various universities, including the University of Windsor.